MEAT

FOR GROWING CHRISTIANS

Frank Hamrick & Jerry Dean

PositiveAction
BIBLE CURRICULUM

Meat: For Growing Christians

Copyright 1972 by Positive Action For Christ, Inc., P.O. Box 700, 502 W. Pippen St., Whitakers, NC 27891. All rights reserved. No part may be reproduced in any manner without permission in writing from the publisher.

Quotations are from the King James Version of the Bible.

17th Printing 2008

Printed in the United States of America

ISBN: 1-929784-23-6

Designed by Shannon Brown
Cover Artwork by Chris Ellison

Published by

TABLE OF CONTENTS

But strong meat belongeth to them that are of full age, even those who by reason of use have their senses exercised to discern both good and evil.
(Hebrews 5:14)

The verse above literally means "solid food belongs to the fully trained athlete who, because of practice, has his senses trained to discern good and evil." Do you really want to become that fully trained athlete and run the race in God's service that He has called you to? Then *Meat* is for you. Babies don't start out eating solid food. Eventually, however, they make the transition to eating meat.

Are you ready to begin your *Meat* diet? Sometimes it will be tough. Often it will be hard to digest. You will have to spend much time in order to get all the good things from *Meat*. But, if you stay with it to the end, you will realize that your spiritual strength has increased more and more with each "meal."

If you're ready to begin, pray right now and ask the Lord by His Spirit to teach you and cause you to become that "fully trained athlete" for Him.

1

THE INSPIRATION OF THE BIBLE— BIBLIOLOGY

That is a question people ask frequently. In fact, some of your unsaved friends probably have already asked you that question. Even some pastors in liberal churches don't think the Bible is inspired.

Definition Of Inspiration

Inspiration means God–breathed. When used in connection with the Scriptures, it means that God breathed into the minds of the writers exactly what He wanted them to say.

| *I've Been Inspired By A Beautiful View Before.* |

That's one type of inspiration, but that's not the same type of inspiration that we have in mind!

Two Types Of Inspiration

Natural Inspiration

This is inspiration on the human level and is caused by psychological and environmental influences on an individual. For instance, due to certain moods and events in one's life, we have various impulses to draw a picture, write a poem, compose a song, play ball, etc. This is not what we mean by biblical inspiration.

Biblical Inspiration

This is inspiration on the heavenly level and is caused by God Himself breathing into a man the actual words He wants man to write. This was purely for the purpose of revelation. God has finished this type of inspiration.

God Has Stopped Inspiring Men To Write The Word Of God

In His last book God had John write a warning. What was it? (Revelation 22:18) _____

_____

You can rest assured that all of God's Word has been revealed by Him. The Book is finished and cannot be added to or taken away from. Yet, Satan continues to attack at this very point!

Satan Attacks The Inspiration Of God's Word

Ask yourself a couple of simple questions:

1. If the Bible is not completely true in every detail, can we know for sure that we are saved? _____

2. Can we trust any part of the Bible if it is incorrect in certain places? _____

If the Bible is not God's Word, then we are poor, ignorant individuals who can know nothing about the life that Christ has to offer. Isn't it logical that the first thing the devil will attack is the truthfulness and trustworthiness of God's Word? _____

_____

7

Defeating Satan's Attacks On The Word Of God

No Errors

First of all, we need to know that the Bible contains no error in its archaeological, scientific, geographic, or historical record. Even though it was written many years before people knew all they know today, it does not contain even one error! Could a book be written by a group of men over different periods of time, about subjects that these men were not experts in, and still be without any error in archaeology, science, history, etc.? _____

There is only one logical way for this to happen: A supernatural power must have directed its writing! If it is not humanly possible for such a book to be written, then a Being who knows everything there is to know must have written the book. Who, then, must have written the Scriptures? _____

Let's look at a second reason why we can be sure the Bible is God's Word.

Fulfilled Prophecy

What about fulfilled prophecies? Everything the Bible has said would happen has happened exactly as prophesied. The Old Testament was written hundreds of years before Christ, and many things were written about Christ even before He was born. Read these verses and tell what was written about Christ many years before He came to earth. Write the answers on the longer lines below.

_____ 1. Isaiah 7:14 _____

_____

_____ 2. Micah 5:2 _____

_____

_____ 3. Zechariah 9:9 _____

_____

_____ 4. Psalm 41:9 _____

_____

_____ 5. Zechariah 11:12–13 _____

_____

_____ 6. Psalm 34:20 _____

_____

_____ 7. Psalm 69:21 _____

_____

_____ 8. Psalm 22:18 _____

_____

_____ 9. Psalm 22:16 _____

_____

_____ 10. Psalm 16:8–11 _____

_____

_____ 11. Psalm 68:18 _____

_____

_____ 12. Psalm 110:1 _____

_____

The following verses record how each of the previous prophecies were fulfilled. Now match the following verses, placing the letter of the correct passage below on the appropriate line above.

A. John 19:31–33	G. Matthew 2:6
B. Matthew 26:15; 27:9–10	H. John 13:18
C. Matthew 1:23	I. Colossians 3:1
D. Matthew 27:34	J. Ephesians 4:7–8
E. Matthew 21:1–6	K. Acts 2:23–27
F. John 20:20, 25	L. Matthew 27:35

- Could all of these prophecies have been fulfilled perfectly if God's Word were not true?_____

Mathematicians tell us that the chances of just the above few prophecies all coming true is 1 out of 2,040! Yet, there are literally hundreds of prophecies in God's Word, all of which came true exactly as God said! The chances of all of them being correct are 1 out of 10 with 300 zeroes behind it! It is mathematically impossible for human prophecy to be so accurate. Conclusion: God's Word is not human, but supernatural.

Thirdly, let's look at what the Bible itself says about the Word of God.

The Bible's Own Testimony

In the Old Testament alone, the phrase "thus saith the Lord" occurs more than 3,800 times! Read these verses and explain in your own words what they mean.

- 2 Peter 1:19–21 _____

_____

_____

- 2 Timothy 3:16 _____

  _____

  _____

- By these two verses we can see that God used men
  to write His Word. However, these men were taught
  (moved) by what? _____

- According to 2 Timothy 3:16, how much Scripture is
  true? _____

Christ's Own Testimony

What did Jesus Himself say about the Word?

- John 10:34–35 _____

  _____

- Matthew 5:18_____

  _____

- Luke 16:17 _____

  _____

Read these statements carefully. If one is true, put a check beside
it; if it is false, put an X beside it and state why it is false.

_____ The Bible contains the Word of God. _____

_____

_____ When you read the Bible, it becomes the Word of
God to you._____

_____

_____ All Scripture that is given by inspiration of God is profitable. _____

_____

_____ The Bible is all the Word of God and every single word is completely true and trustworthy. _____

_____

Complete This Section Without Looking Back At The Lesson

1. What does the word *inspiration* mean when it refers to the Bible? _____

_____

_____

2. Name the two types of inspiration: _____

_____

_____

3. Name four ways we can *know* God's Word is inspired: __

_____

_____

_____

_____

Verses To Memorize

- 2 Peter 1:20–21
- 2 Timothy 3:16

2

WHO IS JESUS CHRIST?—
CHRISTOLOGY

We have just seen that the Bible is completely true and reliable on every subject. There is much talk today about Jesus. But, are all the things people are saying about Him true? Is Christ just a "superstar" or a "big brother" or is He more? Was He just a great teacher and a good man, or was He God in the flesh? Let's see what the Bible says.

> *He's The Lord: God In The Flesh.*

What God's Word Says

- Read John 1:1–2, 14; 1 John 1:1. Who is the "Word" mentioned in these verses? _____

- How long had this Word existed? _____

- Then, we could safely say that Jesus Christ is _____
_____

- John 1:1-2 states that Christ was already in existence in the beginning with God, but then it adds that the Word was_____
_____

- Read Colossians 1:16–17; John 1:3; Ephesians 3:9; and Hebrews 1:1–3. We see by these verses that He _____
_____ and also, by Him _____
_____

- These verses show that Christ is _____
_____

- If Christ were only a big brother or superstar would He be eternal? _____

- Could He have actually created the universe? _____

What Christ Said

- Notice what Christ said about Himself. Read John 10:30; 14:8–9. In your own words state what Jesus said about Himself. _____

_____

_____

His Names Prove His Deity

Match the names of Christ with the Scripture references.

	1. John 1:29	A. The Messiah
	2. John 1:34	B. The Good Shepherd
	3. John 1:41	C. The Lamb of God
	4. John 1:49	D. The Bread of Life
	5. John 10:7-8	E. The Christ, Son of the Living God
	6. John 10:11	F. The Door of the Sheep
	7. John 6:69	G. The Resurrection and the Life
	8. John 14:6	H. The Son of God
	9. John 11:25	I. The Way, Truth, and Life
	10. John 8:12; 9:5	J. The Son of God, King of Israel
	11. John 6:48	K. The Light of the World
	12. John 20:27-29	L. The True Vine
	13. John 15:1	M. Lord and God
	14. Revelation 1:8	N. Alpha and Omega, The Almighty

He Is Either God Or A Liar

Many say that Christ was not God and that He was not the Savior of the world, but He was a great teacher or leader or a good man. If Christ was not God, as He claimed to be, then He was a liar or an insane man! If Jesus Christ is not God, then He is not even a good man!

Other Facts That Prove Christ's Deity

We will now look at several other facts that prove Christ was undoubtedly God in the flesh. Look up these verses and state those things that prove Christ was God.

- Isaiah 7:14; Matthew 1:18; Luke 1:26–27 _____

  _____

  _____

- 1 John 3:5; 2 Corinthians 5:21; Hebrews 4:15 _____

  _____

  _____

- John 20:1–8, 19, 26; 1 Corinthians 15:3–8 _____

  _____

  _____

- How many witnesses do we need to prove something is true? _____

  _____

  _____

- How many people saw Christ alive after His resurrection?

  _____

  _____

Complete This Section Without Looking Back At The Lesson

1. List the facts as well as the Scriptures that prove to your satisfaction that Christ was truly God. _____

   _____

   _____

   _____

   _____

   _____

   _____

   _____

   _____

2. Could Christ not be God and still be a good man?

   _____

3. Prove your answer. _____

   _____

   _____

   _____

   _____

   _____

   _____

Verses To Memorize

- John 20:28–29

3
THE TRINITY — THEOLOGY

You have probably heard a preacher or someone else talk about "the Holy Trinity." Perhaps also you have some vague idea of what is meant by the word *Trinity*. The classic definition of the Trinity is this: "There are three eternal distinctions in one divine essence, known respectively as Father, Son, and Holy Spirit."

What Does That Mean?

It simply means that even though God is only one Being (essence), this one Being exists in three separate persons: the Father, Son, and Holy Spirit.

That's Hard To Believe. I Could Never Explain That.

I can't explain it either! But, if we could figure out God, He wouldn't be much of a God, would He? However, we can offer proof that there is a Holy Trinity, whether we can fully understand it or not.

Proof Of The Trinity

Let's see what the Bible says about this subject.

The Bible Constantly Associates The Three Together In Their Work

1. Read John 6:27b; Romans 1:7; Galatians 1:1; Ephesians 1:2. In each of these verses what two persons are constantly connected together? "God the _____ and _____

2. All three are mentioned at the baptism of Jesus. Note Matthew 3:16–17. In what way do we see each person of the Trinity in this passage?

- The Father _____

  _____

- The Son _____

  _____

- The Holy Spirit _____

  _____

3. How were the disciples to baptize? (Matthew 28:19) "In the name of _____ "

4. Paul's blessing unites the three. Read 2 Corinthians 13:14. "The _____ of the Lord Jesus Christ, and the _____of God, and the _____ of the Holy Spirit be with you all."

5. All three are united in our salvation. Read 1 Peter 1:2 and state what part each plays in our salvation.

- The Father _____

  _____

- The Son _____

  _____

- The Holy Spirit _____

  _____

- To summarize, all three are associated and united in four ways mentioned above. What are they?

  _____

  _____

  _____

  _____

6. All three take part in our spiritual growth. Read 2 Corinthians 3:12-18 and summarize verses 17-18 in your own words. _____

   _____

   _____

   _____

   _____

   _____

Their Eternal Existence Proves The Trinity

1. How long has God the Father existed according to Psalm 90:2? _____

2. What does the Bible say about the Spirit's life–span? (Hebrews 9:14) _____

   _____

3. What does the Bible say about God the Son in John 1:1–2? _____

   _____

Creation Proves The Trinity

1. Read Genesis 1:26. Notice the two pronouns that refer to God used in the verse: _____ and _____. Are these singular or plural? _____

- What does this tell you about God? _____

_____

2. Now, look at John 1:1–3, 14. Who else aided in creation?

_____

- John 1:34 tells us that this other person is called "the
_____"

3. Go back to Genesis 1:2. Who "moved upon the face of the waters" in creation? _____

What Difference Does It Make If I Believe In The Trinity Or Not?

The Trustworthiness Of Christ

1. Read John 14:7–12. Christ says in verse 9, "He that hath seen Me _____"

2. Also, John 10:30 says, " _____
_____"

3. Therefore, if we reject the doctrine of the Trinity, _____ is a liar and cannot be trusted.

Our Faith In The Truthfulness Of God's Word

1. Read 2 Peter 1:20–21. Who wrote the words of God?

_____

- According to verse 21, who "moved" these men in writing the Scriptures? _____

2. Therefore, if we reject the Trinity, we are denying the fact that God wrote the Word! Could we then know for sure that the Bible was true in every detail? _____

The Assurance Of Our Salvation

1. Read 1 John 3:24; 4:13; and Romans 8:14, 16. State in your own words what these verses mean._____

   _____

   _____

   _____

   _____

   _____

2. If we reject the Trinity, can we be sure we're saved? ___

The Enlightening Power Of The Spirit

- Read John 14:26; 15:26. According to these verses what is the work that the "Comforter" (the Holy Spirit) does?

   _____

   _____

   _____

- However, if He is not God, can He honestly tell us the mind of God? _____

- Then, if we deny the doctrine of the Trinity, can we really understand the Scriptures? _____

Brief Summary

The doctrine of the Trinity, simply stated, is that the Holy Spirit is God, Jesus Christ is God, and God the Father is God. They are all three separate, yet they are one God.

Complete This Section Without Looking Back At The Lesson

1. Give the simple definition of the Trinity. _____
    _____
    _____

2. Name three major proofs of the Trinity. _____
    _____
    _____
    _____

3. Name four ways the Bible associates the Three–in–one.
    _____
    _____
    _____
    _____

4. Who created the heavens and the earth and all that is within? (Be specific) _____
    _____

5. What four great truths must we discard if we reject the doctrine of the Trinity? _____
    _____
    _____
    _____

Verses To Memorize

- 2 Corinthians 13:14

- John 1:1–4

4

THE HOLY SPIRIT — PNEUMATOLOGY

We have already seen in an earlier section that the Holy Spirit is a part of the Trinity--He is God. But, there is a great deal of emphasis placed upon the Holy Spirit today, bringing confusion among many. In this chapter we will see what the Bible says about the person and work of the Holy Spirit.

Who Is The Holy Spirit?

His Person

The first thing we must understand is that the Holy Spirit is a person just as Christ and God the Father are persons.

How Can A Spirit Be A Person?

Personality is determined by the possession of:

- Intellect—the ability to think and express thought
- Emotion—the ability to have feelings
- Will—the ability to make decisions and act upon them

- Look at the following verses: Ephesians 4:30; 1 Corinthians 2:10–11; Acts 13:2; and 1 Corinthians 12:11. Which of these verses states that the Spirit has:

    - Intellect _____

    - Emotion_____

    - Will _____

- Proof that the Holy Spirit is a person can be easily found in that the Spirit is *never* referred to as "it," the correct translation should be "He." Read John 16:13–15. How many times is the word "He" used in referring to the Holy Spirit? _____

His Work

Now, let us look at the actual work of the Holy Spirit in conversion. There are four words in the New Testament which indicate the Holy Spirit's work *at* and *after* conversion.

Birth

- Do you remember a verse in the *Milk* booklet that stated all who receive Christ have the right to "become the sons of God"? Where is this verse found? _____

- How do we become actual children in a family on earth?
  _____
  _____

- How do you suppose we are able to become children of God? _____
  _____

- Look at John 3:3. What did Jesus tell Nicodemus was necessary for him to see the kingdom of God? _____
  _____

- What two things in verse 5 did Jesus say we must be "born" of? _____
  _____

- Verse 6 explains verse 5. The first birth or natural birth is a "water birth" because each child spends nine months in water. What then, do the two words in verse 5 mean as explained in verse 6?

  - Water _____
    _____

  - Spirit _____
    _____

- So, we see that we are sons of God because we have been "_____" by the Spirit.

Baptism

- Read 1 Corinthians 12:12–13. These verses tell us that we are all _____ into one body by the Spirit. The word *baptism* means to submerge, to place into.

What Does Baptized Into One Body Mean?

Here's what it means. Again, read carefully Romans 12:4–5; Ephesians 1:19–23; 4:4; 5:23, 30, 32 and Colossians 1:18. Now answer the following questions.

- Who is the "head" spoken of in these verses?_____
  _____

- What is the "body" spoken of in these verses? _____
  _____

- What is the "church"? _____
  _____

- How many people have been baptized (placed) into this
  body? _____

- Now, read again 1 Corinthians 12:12–13 very carefully.
  State in your own words, according to these verses, what
  it means to be baptized into one body by the Spirit.___
  _____
  _____
  _____
  _____

Indwelling

- Read Romans 8:9, 11; 1 Corinthians 3:16; and 1 John
  3:24. According to these verses we are " _____ "
  by the Spirit. Read 1 Corinthians 6:19–20. According to
  these verses where does the Holy Spirit live? _____
  _____

- Thus, what is your body (read carefully)?_____
  _____

- Does your body belong to yourself? _____

- Then, to whom does it belong?_____

- Thus, in light of this, how is a Christian to live? (Be specific) _____
  _____
  _____

Filling

- The fourth word we want to consider concerning the work of the Holy Spirit is found in Ephesians 5:18. Here we are commanded to be " _____ " with the Holy Spirit.

The word *filled* means to be controlled by the Spirit. The literal translation of this verse reads, "Be constantly, moment by moment, controlled by the Holy Spirit."

- Now, let's look again at the four words that describe the Holy Spirit's work. List them.

    1. _____

    2. _____

    3. _____

    4. _____

- If we are born by the Spirit, can we ever be any less born into God's family? _____

- If we are baptized into the body of Christ which is the _____ can we ever become more baptized? _____

- The baptism of the Spirit occurs _____ time and that is at the moment we do what? (Ephesians 1:13-14) _____

- If the Holy Spirit dwells within us, would He ever leave us? (Hebrews 13:5; Matthew 28:20) _____

- However, a Christian who is filled can be less filled at times! How? _____
_____

In other words, we *always* have *all* of Him, but He doesn't always have *all* of us! Are you right now "filled," completely filled, with the Holy Spirit? What areas of your life have you not yielded to Him? _____

- Finally, let's see what can keep a person from being completely filled with the Holy Spirit (in order that we might avoid it!). Read Acts 2:1–4. When the Holy Spirit first came upon the Christians, in what form did He come? (v. 3)
_____
_____

- Fire! He came as an all-consuming fire in their lives! Now read 1 Thessalonians 5:19. Here we are told to " _____ not the Holy Spirit of God." In your own life, how have you quenched or put out, as water on a flame, the Holy Spirit's working in your life?
_____
_____

- Read Ephesians 4:30. " _____ not the Holy Spirit of God." Since the Holy Spirit is a real person, He can be grieved. You can grieve Him as you would grieve your mother or father. Read Ephesians 4:25–32 and list all the things that grieve the Holy Spirit. _____
_____
_____
_____
_____

Christian, examine your heart right now! Is the Holy Spirit filling you? Is He controlling every area of your entire life? Or, has His working been quenched or His person grieved by your own rebellion against Him?

Complete This Section Without Looking Back At The Lesson

1. List at least two verses that prove the Holy Spirit to be a person._____

   _____

2. Are we ever correct to refer to the Holy Spirit as "it"? _____ Why? _____

   _____

   _____

3. List four words that describe the work of the Holy Spirit and describe what each means.

   • _____

     _____

   • _____

     _____

   • _____

     _____

   • _____

     _____

4. When is a person born of the Spirit? _____

   _____

5. When is a person baptized by the Spirit? _____

   _____

6. When is a person indwelt by the Spirit? _____

   _____

7. When is a person filled with the Spirit? _____

   _____

Verses To Memorize

- Ephesians 5:18

- Ephesians 4:30

- 1 Corinthians 6:19–20

5

MAN—
ANTHROPOLOGY

"Man is essentially a good creature. Each man possesses a spark of divinity which can be fanned into flames of goodness by the proper environment. To improve man, we must first improve his education and his living conditions."

You have probably heard this statement. Maybe you haven't heard it quite that way, but you have no doubt heard similar statements. In this chapter we are going to see exactly what the Bible says concerning man's nature.

Adam And Eve

A Perfect Environment

- First, God created a beautiful garden, Eden, a perfect environment. Read Genesis 1:1–25. Pay special attention to verses 10, 12, 18, 21, and 25. What one phrase occurs each time in these verses? _____

  _____

A Perfect Man

- Next, in this perfect environment God made man. Read Genesis 1:26–27 and 2:7. What do we learn about man from these verses? _____

  _____
  _____
  _____

A Perfect Woman

- In chapter 2:21–25, we are told of Eve's creation. Here we have a perfect man and woman in the _____

of _____, in a perfect environment
because God saw that _____
_____

Adam's Duties

- Notice, also, one thing Adam had to do in the garden.
  Genesis 2:15. _____

- Read Genesis 2:16–17 and state the one thing Adam was
  forbidden to do._____

- According to verse 17, what was man's punishment if he
  broke God's commandment? _____

Adam's Sin And Its Effects

You know what happened in chapter 3. Adam and Eve were
tempted by Satan and broke God's commandment. Now note
the effects of Adam's sin.

It Affected Man's Relationship To God

- How did it affect man's relationship to God? (Genesis
  3:23–24)_____
  _____
  _____

It Affected Man's Perfectly Created Nature

- He once walked unashamedly in fellowship with God.
  Now what did man try to do? (Genesis 3:8–10) _____
  _____
  _____

It Affected Man's Body

- How did it affect man's body? (Genesis 3:19; Romans 5:12; and 1 Corinthians 15:22) _____

_____

_____

_____

It Affected Man's Environment

- How did it affect man's environment? (Genesis 3:14, 17–19) _____

_____

_____

_____

You may think, "Yeah, but I didn't sin in the garden! Why do I suffer because of something my ancestors did hundreds of years ago?"

- What tragic results sin brought upon man! We don't know everything that happened as a result of Adam's disobedience, but we do know that every person since Adam has been under God's condemnation! Read Romans 5:12–21. In these verses there is a parallel drawn between what two people? _____

- Keep that parallel in mind. Fill in this blank and then explain the statement. (Romans 5:14) "Adam...is the _____ of him that was to come."

_____

_____

_____

- According to verse 12, what entered the world by one man? _____ and _____.

- Now, read verses 17–19. Verse 19 especially states that by one man's disobedience we were made _____; but also, by one man's _____ we shall be made _____.

Adam was the world's first unrighteous man and passed his death to us. Christ, being God, came and lived as the world's first righteous man and gave His life for us.

- Read the following Scriptures and state in your own words man's condition before God (Romans 3:9–19, 23; Romans 7:18; Isaiah 1:4–6; 53:6; Jeremiah 17:9). _____

  _____

  _____

  _____

  _____

The Answer To Man's Problems

- Men today are making great efforts to cure the problems of the world. Poverty, war, crime, drug abuse, etc. can all be eliminated by better education, better housing, or more money, they say. But is man's real problem an outward or an inward deficiency?_____

- According to the Bible, what is the one basic cause of all of man's problems? _____

- Is this an outward or an inward problem? _____

- Can it be cured outwardly or inwardly? _____

- What is the first step that needs to be taken to solve man's problems? _____

- What is the only cure for sin? _____

- Thus, the real cure for the problems of man is _____
_____

Remember: Peace cannot come without Christ. Peace must be achieved inwardly. The cessation of war won't bring peace. Man must stop war with God by receiving Christ as his Lord and Savior before he will ever realize inward peace.

Complete This Section Without Looking Back At The Lesson

1. Name the four areas in which Adam's sin had an effect.

   _____

   _____

   _____

   _____

2. In what condition was man originally created? _____

   _____

3. What brought about man's fall?_____

4. Are man's problems outward or inward? _____

5. What caused all of man's problems? _____

6. Will the betterment of education and improved housing and living conditions answer man's problems and cure the problems of war, hate, pollution, etc.? _____

- Why or why not?_____

_____

_____

_____

Verses To Memorize

- Romans 5:12

- 1 Corinthians 15:22

- Jeremiah 17:9

6

SATAN—ANGELOLOGY

Perhaps all of us have seen in the paper or on television a character wearing a red suit and having a pitchfork and horns. He's sort of a joke, just to pull tricks on people. This character is called Satan or the devil and sometimes he's referred to as Lucifer.

Who Is Satan Anyway? Is He A Person Or An Influence?

Satan Before The Fall

Turn to Ezekiel 28:12–19 and Isaiah 14:12–17.

His Origin

- What does Ezekiel 28:13–15 tell us about the origin of this creature? _____
  _____

His Appearance

- What did he look like? _____
  _____

His Name

- Isaiah 14:12 tells us his name is _____
  Note: Lucifer means "light bearer" or "the brilliant one."

- He is also called the anointed _____ (Ezekiel 28:14).

His Position

Verses 14 and 15 of Ezekiel 28 also tell us that he was "perfect in his ways," and he is called the "cherub that covereth." This means that Lucifer was the highest ranking creature in God's creation. He was the one nearest the throne of God. In all his beauty he continually praised God.

Satan's Sin

- Read Isaiah 14:12–14 and describe in your own words what happened to Satan and why it happened._____

_____

_____

_____

_____

_____

We now know that Satan was created; he was the greatest among God's creation; he revolted against God and was cast out of heaven.

- Now, 2 Corinthians 11:14 tells us that Satan is an ____

_____

Where Is Satan Now? In Hell?

- Turn to Job 1:6–7. Here we see Satan coming before God and God asks him, "From whence comest thou?" What was Satan's answer? _____

_____

- Read Ephesians 2:2; John 12:31; 14:30. What is Satan called in these passages? _____

Look up the following Scriptures and fill in what Satan is now doing as prince and god of this world.

- Revelation 12:9 _____

  _____

- Zechariah 3:1; 1 Thessalonians. 2:18 _____

  _____

- Matthew 13:19; 2 Corinthians 4:4 _____

  _____

- 2 Thessalonians 2:9 _____

  _____

- 2 Corinthians 11:14_____

  _____

- John 8:44 _____

  _____

- 1 Peter 5:8 _____

  _____

Overcoming Satan

Satan is a very powerful individual. Although he isn't nearly as powerful as God, he is much too strong for you and me. Satan also has followers who do his bidding. (We will see in the next chapter who these followers are.) There's only one way to overcome Satan.

- Note 1 Peter 5:8–9. We must be _____ and _____ (watchful, alert). We must _____ in the faith. This means that God's Word alone will defeat him. That's why it is so important to know the Word!

Satan Seems To Be Winning, And God Seems To Be Losing!

- Turn to Revelation 20:10. State in your words what the Lord will finally do with Satan. _____

_____

_____

Complete This Section Without Looking Back At The Lesson

1. Where did Satan come from? _____

_____

2. What was he like before he fell into sin? _____

_____

_____

3. What was Satan's purpose before his fall? _____

_____

4. In what way did Satan sin? _____

_____

5. What happened to Satan as a result of sin? _____

_____

6. What is Satan doing now? _____

_____

_____

7. How should we treat the devil today? _____

   _____

8. What is his final destiny? _____

Verses To Memorize

- 1 Peter 5:8–9

7

DEMONS— DEMONOLOGY

We have just seen that Satan is a created being. This means that he is existing under the permission of God. Also, it means that he is not all-powerful as God is, he does not know all things as God does, and he cannot be all places at once as God can.

You may be thinking, "But, it seems that Satan is in every city and country in the world! If he cannot be everywhere at once, who causes all this evil?"

- Turn to Revelation 12:7-9. This passage again refers to Satan's fall from heaven. But, notice the last part of verse 9. What does this tell us about his fall?_____
  _____

These "angels," the number of which we do not know, became what the Bible calls "demons" or "devils" (James 2:19; Revelation 9:20).

What Are Demons Like? I've Never Seen One!

- Read Matthew 8:16 and Revelation 16:14. Here, these fallen angels are called_____

- What does Luke 24:39 tell us about spirits? _____
  _____

We also know that even though demons are spirits, they are personalities who possess feelings and have wills of their own.

- Describe the action of the demons in Acts 19:13-16.__
  _____
  _____

Remember: Since demons are spirits, they cannot be seen by humans, but they are still just as real as if they were visible.

- Read Ephesians 6:11–12. According to this passage we see that Christians face more than just a personal devil! We are in a warfare against _____

  _____

- To what do you think "principalities, powers," etc. refer?

  _____

  _____

These are real beings who have personalities, feelings, power, mobility and intelligence! Have you ever tried to fight someone you could not see? How could you possibly win that fight? We must be able to see what demons do and how they act in order to recognize them!

The Work Of Demons

They Seduce

- Read 1 Timothy 4:1–2. Here demons are characterized as being seducers. What does "seducing" mean? _____

  _____

  _____

- Thus, demons in the last days will do what to mankind?

  _____

  _____

- According to these verses, what else will demons do? __

  _____

  _____

They Preach False Doctrine

- Read 2 Corinthians 11:13–15. Do demons influence and even possess some preachers? _____

According to 1 Timothy 4:1–2 you will remember that some will "give heed" to the "doctrines of demons." So, every person who talks about the Bible and about Jesus Christ is not necessarily of God!

But, How Can I Tell A True Minister Of God From A Minister Of Satan?

- Turn to 1 John 4:1–3. Are we to believe every spirit (that is, every preacher)? _____

  - Why? _____

- What is the test of a true minister and a false one? ___
  _____
  _____
  _____

A word of explanation is in order: 1 John 4:2–3 is talking about more than just the fact that true ministers believe that Jesus came to the earth. It is calling this Jesus, who came to earth, The Christ, that is in question here. Even Satan's ministers will admit that Jesus was a human being who was on this earth 2000 years ago. What they will not admit, however, is that this same Jesus is God Himself! They say He was "like God" or He "came from God," but they will not admit that He was almighty God in the flesh! This, again, is why we must beware of a lot of "Jesus" talk! Much of it is centered on the humanity of Christ and not His Deity.

Beware! Watch out for those who talk of "Jesus the Man," who emphasize His tears, His hunger, His poverty, and other aspects of His humanity, almost to the exclusion of His Deity!

- Note 1 John 2:22. What does God call a man who denies that Jesus (the person) is the Christ (God in the flesh)?

  _____

What Else Can Demons Do?

From all that we have studied thus far, we can see that some people today are actually possessed by demons!

- Do you think a Christian can be indwelt by a demon?

  _____

  - Why? _____

    _____

    _____

    _____

Christians can be demon influenced, however! A person, though born–again, can "fool around" with these evil spirits until they begin to influence his thinking and cause him to do things he normally would not do.

- Read 1 Thessalonians 5:22. What are we told to do in this passage? _____

  _____

  _____

- What does that verse mean? _____

  _____

  _____

- Demons are involved in many things today which Christians should avoid. Note Deuteronomy 18:9–11 and list those things which are said to be "abominations."

  _____

  _____

  _____

- Match the following present day practices to the proper abomination listed above.

  - Astrology_____

  - Ouija Boards, Tarot Cards _____

  - Palm Reader _____

  - Talking to the Dead _____

- Should Christians become involved in such things?___

- Do we need to consult such things for guidance?_____

- What do we, as Christians, have for guidance and enlightenment in making decisions and plans? _____

  _____

  _____

If Demons Have So Much Power, How Can We Ever Defeat Them?

- Turn back to Ephesians 6:12. Now read verses 13–17 and especially note verses 16–17. What does Paul say "above all" we're to use to defeat Satan and his forces?

  1. _____

2. _____

3. _____

Are you really using God's weapons in this battle against your spiritual enemies, or are you trying to win the battle your own way? Maybe you've decided by now that you just can't win-- you've already quit! Maybe you're right now fooling around with those things you listed earlier. Remember, you are "kept by the power of God." Is He not able to keep you from these things if you will only let Him? Stay close to the Lord; He's the only one who can keep us true and faithful.

Are Drugs A Gateway For Demons To Influence Us?

- Read Revelation 9:21; 18:23; 21:8 and 22:15. You will note the use of one word in all four passages. What is it?

  _____

- The word *sorcery* is actually the word *pharmaceutical* and literally means drugs. Sorcery and witchcraft are linked together in Isaiah 47:9 and Acts 8:9. According to Acts 8:9, what was Simon doing with drugs? _____

  _____

  _____

- Therefore, should any Christian get involved in the mis-use of drugs? _____

  - Why? _____

    _____

    _____

Complete This Section Without Looking Back At The Lesson

1. What were demons originally? _____

2. How did they become demons? _____
_____

3. Describe the appearance of demons. _____
_____
_____
_____

4. Name at least two things that demons do that are related to truth. _____
_____
_____

5. How can you tell a true minister from a false one?
_____
_____

6. Name some of the activities in which demons are involved today. _____
_____
_____
_____

7. What three things does Paul say we are to use to defeat Satan and his forces? _____
_____
_____

Verses To Memorize

- Ephesians 6:10–12

8

THE SECOND COMING— ESCHATOLOGY

Although this is the last study of the *Meat* booklet, it is certainly not the least important. This chapter may be the greatest and most blessed of the entire booklet. You are now going to see what the Bible says about the second coming of the Lord Jesus Christ! It is thrilling to know, if we are saved, that one day the Lord God Himself will return to earth!

Maybe you've heard someone say something like this, "Everybody is always talking about Jesus coming! They've been saying that for hundreds of years and He still hasn't come! I say it's all a big joke." The Bible talks about that kind of person. Read 2 Peter 3:3-4.

But How Do I Know That He Will Really Return Some Day?

- Turn to Acts 1:8-11. Who is speaking in verse 8? _____

  _____

- To whom is He saying these things? _____

- What happened after He said these things? _____

  _____

- There are two key words in verse 11 that will teach us a lot. One is the word *same*. What does it mean to say, "this same Jesus...shall come again"?_____

  _____

  _____

- Was Jesus' body a physical or spiritual one at the time He left the earth? _____Then how will this same Jesus return? _____

  _____

  _____

- The second key word is *like manner*. Explain in your own words the phrase "this same Jesus shall come in like manner as ye have seen Him go into heaven." _____

  _____

  _____

Will He Come In The Air Or Return To Earth?

Two Aspects Of His Second Coming

Keep in mind that Christ's second coming is in two parts! First, He will come in the air, and later He will return to the earth.

The Rapture

- Turn to 1 Thessalonians 4:16–17 (read very carefully). Who are the "dead in Christ"? _____

  _____

- When will they arise? _____

  _____

- What will happen to Christians who are "alive and remain"? _____

  _____

- Where will these two groups meet the Lord according to verse 17? _____

This part of Christ's return is called the Rapture of the church. The word *rapture* literally means *caught up*.

Will The Unsaved Go Up As Well?

- Read 1 Thessalonians 4:16 again. Who shall rise first?
  _____

- Not just "the dead," but the dead in Christ! What does that mean?_____
  _____
  _____

If only the dead "in Christ" arise, what happens to the dead who are not in Christ? Where are they when all of this happens? What happens to them?

- Read Luke 16:22–23 and answer the above questions by noting where the rich man was. _____
  _____
  _____
  _____

Since the dead "in Christ" go up at the Rapture while the dead out of Christ stay in hell at the Rapture, we can draw some conclusions concerning those who are alive at the Rapture.

- What will happen to Christians who are "alive and remain" when the Rapture takes place? (1 Thessalonians 4:17)
  _____
  _____

- What can we assume happens to those who are alive at the rapture, but are not "in Christ"? _____
  _____
  _____
  _____

Can My Body Live Outside The Earth's Atmosphere?

- Read 1 Corinthians 15:51–53. According to these verses what will happen to all Christians' bodies?_____

  _____

  _____

- What does the phrase *put on immortality* mean? ____

  _____

  _____

- So, we see a few basic facts about the Rapture. When will it occur? (Matthew 24:44) _____

  _____

- Who will be involved? (John 14:3; 1 Thessalonians 4:16–17)_____

  _____

- Where will we meet Christ? (1 Thessalonians 4:17)___

  _____

What Will Happen To Those Left On Earth?

- They will endure seven horrible years known as the Tribulation. Matthew 24:21–22 describes that period of time. What is the time period called? (verse 21) _____

  _____

- What is stated about that time (in your own words)?__

  _____

  _____

  _____

During this period the Holy Spirit will not be present because He will be caught up with the church. Satan will be free to do what he pleases! Sin will completely prevail and God will pour out His wrath upon the earth. What a terrible time of judgment!

Match the passage with the event that will occur.

	1. Terrible sores upon men	A. Revelation 16:3
	2. Men scorched with the sun	B. Revelation 16:2
	3. Sea turned to blood	C. Revelation 16:8
	4. Darkness on the earth	D. Revelation 16:10
	5. Rivers turned to blood	E. Revelation 16:4
	6. Terrible earthquakes	F. Revelation 16:17–20
	7. 90 lb. hailstones	G. Revelation 16:21

What Will Happen When Christ Does Come Back To Earth?

The Revelation

Keep in mind that Christ will come in the air (the Rapture) and will take all the saved, both dead and alive, to be with Him in heaven. Those who are left will endure seven horrible years of judgment (the Tribulation), after which the Lord will then return to the earth (the Revelation).

- Now note what will happen. Read Matthew 24:30–31; Luke 21:27. Who will see Christ coming? (Remember who will be on earth at that time.) _____

_____

_____

- What will they do when they see Him coming? _____

_____

- Keep verse 31 in mind. Turn to Jude 14 and Zechariah 14:5. Who will come with the Lord at this time? _____

_____

- To what place will Christ return? (Zechariah 14:4) ____

_____

- What will happen to Satan? (Revelation 20:1–3) _____

_____

For 1000 years Christ and His saints will live and rule on the earth. This is called the Millennial Reign of Christ.

- Now read Revelation 20:7–10 and state in your own words what will happen. _____

_____

_____

_____

_____

What Happens To The Unsaved At The End Of The 1000 Year Reign?

- Read Revelation 20:11-15. State in your own words what will happen. _____
_____
_____
_____
_____

What a sad and terrible day for those who have never trusted Christ. They must then spend eternity, forever burning, in the Lake of Fire. How tragic!

Complete This Section Without Looking Back At The Lesson

1. Define the following terms as to what they represent in future world events:

   - The Rapture_____
   _____

   - The Tribulation _____
   _____

   - The Millennial Reign _____
   _____

   - The Revelation _____
   _____

2. Put each of these four events in their proper order of occurrence. _____
_____

3. What are the two aspects of the second coming of Christ?
_____
_____

4. Who will be caught up in the Rapture? _____

_____

5. Explain what happens to our bodies at the Rapture and give a verse to prove your statement. _____

_____

_____

6. Name at least three differences in the Rapture and the Revelation of Christ: _____

_____

_____

_____

_____

_____

7. What will be the final abode of the unsaved? Give a verse to prove your answer. _____

_____

_____

Verses To Memorize

- Acts 1:11

- 1 Thessalonians 4:16–17

EXAMINATION
QUESTIONS

Complete the following questions without looking back in your book for answers.

1. What does the word *inspiration* mean?_____

   _____

2. Name four major proofs that the Bible is the inspired Word of God. _____

   _____

   _____

   _____

3. Name the two types of inspiration._____

   _____

   _____

4. Quote 2 Timothy 3:16 from memory. _____

   _____

   _____

   _____

5. What do we mean when we speak of the deity of Jesus Christ?_____

   _____

6. List three names of Christ that prove He is God. _____

   _____

   _____

7. Quote John 20:28–29 from memory. _____

   _____

   _____

   _____

   _____

8. Give the simple definition of the Trinity. _____

   _____

   _____

9. Name three major proofs of the Trinity. _____

_____

_____

_____

10. What four great truths must we discard if we reject the doctrine of the Trinity? _____

_____

_____

_____

11. List two verses that prove the Holy Spirit to be a person.

_____

_____

12. List four words that describe the work of the Holy Spirit and describe what each means. _____

_____

_____

_____

_____

13. State when each of the following happens:

- The new birth _____

- The baptism of the Spirit _____

- The indwelling of the Spirit _____

- The filling of the Spirit _____

14. Quote 1 Corinthians 6:19–20 from memory. _____

_____

_____

_____

_____

_____

15. Name the four areas in which Adam's sin had an effect.

_____

_____

_____

_____

16. What brought about man's fall? _____

17. Are man's problems outward or inward? _____
    How do you know? _____

    _____

18. What is the only real cure for man's problems? _____

    _____

19. What was Satan like before he sinned?_____

    _____

    _____

20. In what way did Satan sin (give reference)? _____

    _____

    _____

21.What is Satan doing now? _____

    _____

    _____

22. How should we treat the devil today?_____

    _____

23. Quote 1 Peter 5:8–9 from memory. _____

    _____

    _____

    _____

    _____

    _____

24. Where did demons come from? _____

_____

25. How can you tell a true preacher from a false one? ____

_____

_____

_____

26. Name three things Paul says we are to use to defeat Satan and his forces. _____

_____

_____

_____

27. Define what will happen during each of the following:

- The Rapture_____

_____

- The Tribulation _____

_____

- The Revelation _____

_____

28. What are the two aspects of the second coming of Christ?

_____

_____

_____

29. Name at least three differences in the Rapture and the Revelation of Christ. _____

_____

_____

_____

30. Each doctrine studied in this booklet goes by a theological term that is listed with the title of each chapter. List each chapter and its theological name. We have listed the first title for you.

- The Inspiration of the Bible—Bibliology

- _____

- _____

- _____

- _____

- _____

- _____

- _____

31. Give one verse that teaches each of the following doctrines:

- The inspiration of the Bible _____

- The Deity of Jesus Christ _____

- That God the Father, Son, and Holy Spirit are three, yet one God_____

- That man is a sinner and must die _____

- That Christ is coming back _____